CW00658759

what's your excuse
for not
succeeding as an artist

what's your excuse ...

SUCCEEDING
AS AN
ARTIST?

**Overcome your excuses, nurture your
creative potential and thrive**

deborah henry-pollard

"Deborah's writing is straightforward and pragmatic, with her years of accumulated knowledge hitting the nail on the head time and time again. It's as if she knows exactly what the reader is thinking and addresses internal dialogue with practical solutions that are applicable to creative folks at all stages of their career. Take my word for it: once you start reading, you won't want to stop"

Susan J Mumford, entrepreneur, speaker and author, founder of Be Smart About Art and the Association of Women Art Dealers

"I am completely blown away by Deborah's book! It has a really concise, engaging and understandable writing style. It is really refreshing. All chapters are valid and helpful: the exercises are great and point the reader in the right direction. I really enjoyed reading it and have already started with a few of the exercises. Knowing Deborah, I could hear her reading it: it reflects who she is and her style"

Christine Manderla, artist

"Let's be honest... it's pretty scary to become a professional artist. You need to be vulnerable and confident, determined and very motivated as well as a listener and observer. And you need to be a multi-tasker doing very different jobs – not just in terms of developing your creative skills, but also in pricing your work and getting the word out. Plenty of opportunities for your worries to take over and play less than big. I love Deborah's approach as it covers soooo many of the worries that we might have as creatives. Some will be bigger than others, and some you might not even have realised that you have! She gets you thinking. She gets you smiling at yourself. She gets you to take action. And throughout this book she shows her deep understanding and love for art and artists"

Patricia van den Akker, director of The Design Trust

"Deborah demystifies jargon and holds your hand while you face individual fears, and lets you know that you are not alone in taking that first step on your creative journey. It is irrelevant whether you have taken the perceived first step before. You can't change the past but can make 'right now' the start of something new and exciting and Deborah's book gives you the tools to step out with confidence on any creative path you choose.

She gives great examples – it's reassuring to know that historical 'successful' figures also had struggles and used personal tips and tricks to help them develop their creative passions and visions. A great reminder that the creative process is a journey and not a 'one hit wonder'.

The power you get from knowing you are not alone in your apprehension in starting something new *is amazing. Insecurities and perceived barriers swiftly start to feel a bit silly, which means the challenge of taking a 'first step' becomes absolutely manageable"*

Kate Enters, artist, founder and director of ArtCan

"This book is very well written, with wise and useful advice, illustrated with great examples, exercises and personal experience. I am a coach and an artist, and this book is spot on"

Sharon Baker, artist and executive coach

"This book is very comprehensive. Often backed up by the author's own experiences, ideas as to how to move forward are clearly stated, as are subsequent exercises and tips. Exercises are presented in both a reader-friendly and user-friendly manner, making it easy to follow a process step by step.

I've taken a number of suggestions and motivational quotes from throughout the book, assigned each one to a single piece of paper and bound them together in a booklet which is set to hang above my desk. The suggestions as to how to create and maintain a vision were ones that really struck a positive chord. I shall be using these! Love the kick starting exercise too - such fun!

Very useful and inspirational content"

Sarah Hartley-Edwards, artist

Also in this series

What's Your Excuse for not Succeeding as an Artist?

This first edition published in 2018 by WYE Publishing
9 Evelyn Gardens, Richmond TW9 2PL
www.wyepublishing.com

Copyright © Deborah Henry-Pollard 2018

Deborah Henry-Pollard asserts her moral right to be identified as
the author of this book

ISBN 978-1-9999868-0-3

Cover and text design by Annette Peppis & Associates

*All rights reserved. No part of this publication may be
reproduced, stored in a retrieval system or transmitted in any
form or by any means, electronic, mechanical, photocopying,
recording or otherwise, without the prior permission of the
publishers*

'What's Your Excuse…?' is a UK Registered Trade Mark
(Registration No: 3018995)

www.whatsyourexcuse.co.uk
Follow What's Your Excuse…? on Twitter – @whats_yr_excuse
www.facebook.com/whatsyourexcusebooks

www.catching fireworks.co.uk
Follow Deborah on Twitter – @fireworksdhp
www.facebook.com/CatchingFireworks/

Contents

Introduction

How this book will help you

As an artist, you are driven to create; creativity is in every fibre of your being and you can't fight it. In some ways you are already successful every time you pick up a pencil and draw.

You may love to create art in your spare time, you may be on the brink of starting an artistic career or you may have already exhibited and sold work but don't know how to progress to the next level.

The theory of setting up as a professional artist is simple enough, but you may be struggling to put that theory into practice. I know many talented artists who do.

Whatever stage you're at in your own artistic journey I've written this book to help you to develop and thrive doing the thing you love, so that you can get the recognition (and the income) you deserve.

In this book I will help you to understand and address the thoughts, doubts and beliefs which we can allow to get in our way, preventing us from developing and enjoying our creative lives. As a creative coach I regularly hear clients and art world professionals express a wide range of doubts and perceived problems and obstacles. From my work with them I know that it's possible to overcome mental barriers and perceived obstacles in order to succeed.

What is success?

At this point it's worth exploring the meaning of success. In my experience success means different things to different people. It's important for you to know what it means to you.

For some people success means wealth, fame, awards, possibly a title or a place at the top table of the art world.

For others, wealth and fame isn't what they want their lives to be about. What motivates them is the desire to express themselves and to feel the satisfaction of being who they were born to be. But they get stuck because wealth and fame is what they think they 'should' be aiming for, what the world seems to celebrate and what business books tell us we should be working towards.

The Oxford English Dictionary defines success as 'the accomplishment of an aim or purpose'. That's it, and it could apply equally to a glittering career or making a decent cup of tea.

Maya Angelou reputedly said that success is liking yourself, liking what you do and liking how you do it.

American entrepreneur Tony Hawk says, 'My definition of success is doing what you love. I feel many people do things because they feel they have to and are hesitant to risk following their passion'.[1]

As a coach, I personally measure my own success by the feeling I get when working with exciting and inspiring people. There is a practical aspect of my work where I have to generate an income, but only because it allows me to do more of the work I love.

So forget what you think other people mean by success and define it in your terms. What do you want your own unique, thriving, creative life to be?[2]

Then you can go for it.

---

1   Tony Hawk interviewed by Gary Cohn, Entrepreneur Magazine, October 2009
2   Check out Martyn Lewis's book Reflections on Success (CB Creative Books, 2014) for a collection of interviews with sixty-seven famous people on what success means to them

The benefits of pursuing success

The benefits of pursuing and enjoying more success might seem obvious, but I think it's important to keep these in mind to motivate yourself.

The benefits of having a successful and thriving artistic practice include:

- Creating a career and lifestyle from your vocation
- Creating a career and lifestyle which is individual to you
- Doing what inspires you and being inspired by what you do
- Having the opportunity to express yourself
- A feeling of wellbeing: the arts can help keep you well, aid recovery and enable longer lives better lived by easing the physical and mental challenges of ageing[3]
- Broadening your world view by seeing the world through art

---

3   *All-Party Parliamentary Group on Arts, Health & Wellbeing –
Creative Health: The Arts for Health & Wellbeing
http://www.artshealthandwellbeing.org.uk/appg-inquiry*

- Opportunities for collaborations with new contacts and networks
- Continuing artistic stimulation, adding spice and excitement to your life

Above all, there is the immense gratification of doing something for the sheer pleasure of it.

And what if you don't follow your artistic instincts? As a coach, I sometimes find myself working with people who seem to have it all in traditional, professional careers – accountants, lawyers and academics – but who are all living their lives to comply with other people's expectations. This is fine if you want to measure your success against someone else's values. But it can be destructive, leaving you feeling unfulfilled, trapped, unhappy and out of balance because your life is running counter to your own values and sense of self-worth.

So this is your chance to decide – how can you develop your creativity to improve your life?

How to use this book

Whether a thought, doubt or belief seems like a boulder in the road or a stone in your shoe, it is hindering your progress. This book aims to help you clear a path to the success you desire.

So what are the barriers stopping you?

And how many of those barriers are real? I mean, *really* real?

We can believe something is a barrier because, for example:

- We haven't taken the time to think beyond the obvious
- We don't have a necessary skill
- We 'know' we can't do something, even though we haven't even tried it
- We don't have the materials or tools
- We don't have the time

Neurosurgeon Dr Ben Carson believes that, 'If we choose to see the obstacles in our path as barriers, we stop trying. If we choose to see the obstacles as hurdles, we can leap over them. Successful people don't have fewer problems. They have determined that nothing will stop them from going forward'.[4]

This book addresses perceived barriers. Take it one chapter at a time and work on one barrier at a time. Pick the one which resonates most with you. Then move on to the next one.

Before you know it, who knows what barriers you will have broken through?

---

4   Ben Carson, *Gifted Hands: The Ben Carson Story*, Zondervan, 1986

The Excuses

Fears

I'm frightened

I want to make it clear that I don't dismiss any fear, large or small, as silly or unimportant. A doctor once told me that when you are in a frightened state, for whatever reason, it is your fear and it is very real. The key is to have the fear but to not let the fear have you.

The first time you try something it's natural to be fearful. Indeed, as poet and creative coach Mark McGuinness says, 'When you set yourself a big challenge, you should expect the fear to rise up before you. You should look out for it and even welcome it – because if you don't experience much fear, it's not much of a dream'.[5] Fear and excitement are two sides of the same emotional coin, showing that something is important to you. Dame Judi Dench is open about her life-long stage fright but she uses that fear as fuel: 'Fear engenders a huge amount of energy and you have to make it work for the better, otherwise you'd crumble'.[6]

---

5   *Mark McGuinness, Resilience: Facing Down Rejection and Criticism on the Road to Success, Lateral Action Books 2013*
6   *https://www.stylist.co.uk/people/judi-denchs-advice-to-her-30-year-old-self-from-coping-with-fear-to-subverting-the-norm/22807*

If fear is holding you back don't throw away your idea and settle back into your comfort zone. You don't have to jump with both feet – find a way to dip a toe into the water. You don't have to paint a masterpiece straight away. Start by playing with paints in a sketchbook or sketch with a pencil on a napkin or take snaps on your phone before launching into a photography project. It's perfectly okay to develop your work and expand your comfort zone gradually.

Find a way to dip a toe into the water

It's also worth asking yourself, 'What's the worst that can happen?' I use this question with my coaching clients to explore their perceived fear; to explore why it is frightening and how they can get past it (which may not necessarily be getting rid of the fear, but managing it).

Try it for yourself:

- What are you frightened of? (For example, giving a talk about my work)
- What's the worst that can happen? (I could look foolish)
- Why would that be a problem? (People may think I'm unprofessional)
- What do you need to do to avoid that? (Prepare my talk, know my audience, check my facts, practise, etc)

- And what else could happen? Go back to the first step and continue this process until all of your fears are addressed
- Finish by asking yourself, 'If I do what I fear, what could I achieve?'

Running through this process helps to break down the issue, to make it seem at least surmountable whilst creating the headspace to look for possibilities and pathways.

Sometimes there is no action to be taken: you only need the realisation that the worst that could happen isn't actually that bad. For example, if you do make a fool of yourself (in your own eyes) in front of a group of people you will never meet again, will it matter in six months' time?

If you want to do something as big as giving up your job to follow your dream to create art it is rational to be fearful about the financial consequences, about whether you will be able to run a business or about whether people will like your work. But build up a habit of facing what makes you fearful because the more progress you make and the more small triumphs you experience the more you create resilience for the next time. This is not necessarily about bungee jumping or white water rafting; it could be about walking into a roomful of strangers or picking up the phone to call a new contact.

And often, the worst that can happen is that you miss your chance to do something brilliant.

I don't have the confidence

How often do you tell yourself that you can't do something or that you wouldn't be any good? I expect that you can provide evidence for it as well – the *one* time you made a mistake, the *one* time you tripped over, the *one* time you forgot someone's name. From that, you can doubt and question all of your abilities and worth.

Meanwhile you completely forget the thousands of times you got things absolutely right, walked without mishap and successfully introduced people to each other. You can begin to re-programme yourself to look for the positives: all the great stuff you have done. Confidence can also be about recognising that you have something unique to offer. Not necessarily better, finer, more brilliant that anyone else but simply unique to you.

Also, have you ever experienced that feeling, 'Any moment now they are going to find me out and realise I am a fraud, making it up as I go along?' Me too. This is a recognised condition known as Imposter Syndrome and it hits many of us at some point in our lives.

When this thought rears its ugly head, counter it by creating a Confidence List – ten things you have done which make you feel proud and confident when you think about them. When you feel the doubts hit use this list to remind yourself of who you are at your best.

Your list will be personal to you but examples from clients' lists include:

- Leaving home
- Bringing up a child
- Running a marathon
- Being a great cook
- Planning a fabulous birthday party
- Having a painting in an exhibition
- Making greetings cards which make the recipients feel special
- Learning a language
- Buying a house
- Raising money for a charity
- Making a film
- Writing a short story
- Being a great friend
- Managing a budget

It doesn't matter how big or small the accomplishments are on your list. All that matters is that the list works for you. Remember how that confidence feels and take that feeling into your new project.

You might also want to try the Alphabet Game, which is fun and seemingly frivolous, but which can uncover real nuggets of gold.

Go through the alphabet and for each letter, find a positive word to describe yourself. Like most games, there are rules:

- Go through the list as quickly as possible, giving yourself as little time as possible to think or debate with yourself. It can usually be done in a minute, but no more than two minutes
- All the words must be positive
- Preface every word with 'I am', for example:

  I am amazing

  I am brilliant

  I am courageous

  I am direct

  I am exciting

  And so on…..

I recommend writing out the letters of the alphabet before you start because forgetting which letter comes next can spoil the flow!

The speed generates energy and the 'I am' creates a positive attitude.

You can play this game anywhere, such as on the way to your private view or a meeting about which you are nervous. It gives you a boost and can help distract you from your nerves. You can also capture in a few words how that process felt.

Try it out today – and let me know what you come up with for X and Z!

Each time you do something which requires confidence add it to your Confidence List or your Alphabet Game to build an ever expanding picture of yourself as a confident person. This is one of the great things about confidence – it is something which you can grow day by day through small, steady achievements and actions.

I probably won't be any good at it

Even people who seem to the rest of us to be confident and thriving in their creative work can believe this when they consider beginning new projects or developing new areas of their practice.

They think things like:

* I can't paint because no one would buy from me

- I couldn't run an online shop
- I'd be useless at talking to art dealers
- No one wants the kind of work I do
- I'm not going to try because it will all go wrong

If someone said any of these things to your face, you might think them exceptionally rude. You might ask them who they thought they were, talking to you like that. They would certainly get unfriended on Facebook.

But there is one person who often talks to us like that. Someone we trust. Someone we believe is on our side. Someone we believe only tells us the truth. Our self, or our Inner Critic, that internal voice which makes disparaging and negative remarks, and because this is our own voice we believe the remarks to be true: after all, we wouldn't lie to ourselves.

Would we?

Russ Harris, author of The Happiness Trap, says that eighty percent of our thinking time involves some element of negativity, looking for problems to solve. [7] It becomes problematic when, instead of looking at the negativity as merely one view of a situation, you take it as the truth and, even worse, as damning self-criticism. That horrid little voice can drag you down,

---

7   Russ Harris, The Happiness Trap: How to Stop Struggling and Start Living, Robinson Publishing, 2008

find fault and gloat at your misfortune. It can leave you with unsettling feelings and create a habit of further negative thinking.

The good news is that you *can* break this negative internal conversation. The thoughts can still come up (you are human after all) but you can control what you do with them. Are they constructive comments? Then work with them. If not, stop believing them.

Here's how to do that:

* Instead of accepting your thoughts unconditionally, look on them as opinions which need to be proven before you agree with them
* Imagine the negative voice speaking like Mickey Mouse. Try it now – see, Mickey cannot be taken seriously!
* Regard your chattering mind as a 'trying to be helpful but rather overly-anxious and overly-critical' neighbour. Say, 'Thanks for your input, but I've got this covered'
* Imagine stuffing the negative thoughts into a fireworks tube, lighting it and watching them explode into glorious colours across the sky and out of your life!

Even if there are times when you may need to develop new skills or habits, ignore that inner critic, concentrate on moving forward and stay focused on your big, brilliant idea.

You might also like to take a look at the exercise I've included at the end of this book for more advice on managing your thoughts – Catch It, Check It, Change It.

I don't want to fail

When people talk about their failures, they talk about how things went wrong. But what they usually mean is that they tried something and it didn't work out the way they expected. The 'failure' comes from having an expectation that is not met.

Scientists actually work *with* failure; they *never* expect to succeed the first time round. The steps for a scientific process are:

- Ask a question
- Do background research
- Construct a hypothesis
- Test your hypothesis by doing an experiment
- Analyse your data and draw a conclusion
- Accept or reject the hypothesis and go back to step three

The words 'success' and 'failure' are nowhere to be seen. The idea is to work through all the possibilities, learn from those which don't work and move on to the next one with a bit more knowledge each time.

In 1968 a scientist tried to create a super-strong adhesive. He 'failed' because it had a very low tack but several years and many experiments later his 'failure' was the basis of the first Post-It Notes.[8]

Don't be hard on yourself and expect success every time. Remember what Thomas Edison is famously purported to have said about not failing but just finding ten thousand ways which didn't work.

Embrace and encourage failure as a way of developing ideas, discovering new ways of working, finding out how materials work and stretching your ingenuity through problem solving. You might even discover something you couldn't have imagined.

I might be successful

This may seem like a ridiculous worry – surely the reason you picked up this book is because you want to be successful? But it's a valid concern as success can bring its own problems.

---

8   https://www.post-it.com/3M/en_US/post-it/contact-us/about-us

You may have heard of the concept of the difficult second album or novel. In the US they refer to the 'Sophomore Slump', when the second year in college or second performance or production doesn't live up to the first. You have impressed first time around and suddenly everyone is looking at you eagerly to see what you will produce next. Galleries and clients will be expecting you to deliver the same quality or even better. Some will be excited, wanting to see you reach even greater heights. Others may want to see you crash and burn. There can be a lot to live up to.

Or, if you are successful in one style, you may fear being pigeonholed as a portrait painter, for example, when you want to experiment with abstraction. Whilst some artists do prefer working in a signature style others like Picasso move through different periods (in his case six within twenty-eight years) or different media (he was also a ceramicist, a printmaker and stage designer).

Remind yourself of what success means to you

You might also be worried that if your career takes off you will be overwhelmed with commissions and exhibition offers and you won't have time to work in the way and with the balance you want. You will be swept away by what other people want from you.

Remind yourself of what success means to you.

Money? Working three days a week in the studio? Spending six months travelling every year? Taking off all school holidays to be with your children? Balancing two careers? Create a picture of what your successful, thriving life looks like. Then when people ask or expect you to do things, take a step back and ask yourself, 'Does this fit with what I want, does it offer me an opportunity I would like to take, what does my instinct say?' Remember that you have control over what you want to do and that includes saying a very polite but very emphatic 'no' to anything which doesn't contribute to your aims.

You may also like to refer to "I'm frightened", where you'll find an exercise to help you explore your fears.

Mindset

I'm overwhelmed – my idea is too big

Your ideal project or career may seem impossible because too much needs to happen, or it seems too big a challenge. When something seems too big we can be tempted to give up, perhaps then regretting for the rest of our lives that we never did that 'impossible' thing.

Now let me be clear: I am not one of those people who believe that if you set your sights on something and think enough positive thoughts, it will happen, nor that if it doesn't you obviously didn't want it enough or try hard enough. But I do believe that if we step back from 'it's impossible' we can achieve more than we expect.

It is true that if you try to do everything in one go it may well be impossible. But imagine you are standing at the foot of a mountain and your dream project or career is sitting on the summit. Are you realistically going to reach the top in one mighty leap? Unless you possess superpowers I would guess not.

By taking one small step a day, you will get closer and closer to the top of the mountain. By staying focused on your destination and moving forward consistently you will stay motivated and keep your dream alive. As artist Alex Katz said, 'Everything is in steps. One thing leads to another'.[9] From taking one step at a time he has built a body of work which has been exhibited in over two hundred solo exhibitions and nearly five hundred group exhibitions.

For example, if you want to become skilled with oil paints try starting with some small sketches, then experiment with mixing colours and playing with different size brushes before moving from paper to canvas and building your composition.

Or to build up to making a first film learn how to use the video on your phone, create a two minute continuous video story and learn how to use editing software.

Or to take some steps towards writing a book you could start by writing a hundred words about your cat, build up to an essay, find a writing group or write an outline.

Ask someone you respect for advice (in my experience creative people always want to help and support others to create) and harness the power of YouTube, Google and online groups who won't care how silly a question may seem!

Every so often you may find that your small daily actions build up a momentum or create an opportunity

9   https://www.interviewmagazine.com/art/alex-katz

which is the equivalent of hitching a lift on a cable car.

How can you break your big, 'impossible' project down into doable elements? What is the first step you will take? Today.

I don't have the motivation

If you are struggling to get started, head back to "The benefits of pursuing success". As you read through it, think about how each of those benefits could impact you. Which ones jump out at you? What others can you think of for yourself?

In five years' time, we will all be somewhere. Do you want to choose where you will be or just allow yourself to drift and hope for the best?

Here's a plan if you want to be somewhere else in five years' time:

Create a vision
The benefits of having a vision for your practice include:

* **Having a direction and a purpose**

  Think about planning a holiday. When deciding where to go, you start thinking about different places, imagining what they will be like and what you can do there. Then you choose a destination and start to make concrete plans: how you will travel, how long it will take, where you will stay. How could you plan your holiday if you hadn't had the vision of where you were going? The same goes with your creative practice, however big or small

- **Having a clear message you can communicate to potential collaborators**

  You never know who you are talking to. The theory of six degrees of separation says that you are at most only six people away from the person who could support you in fulfilling your vision. The problem is we don't know how that chain fits together. The person you casually chat with tomorrow could be the indirect key to your future success. Create a synopsis of your vision which can be quickly communicated and you can enrol everyone you meet in helping you to reach it

- **Heightened awareness to opportunities**

  How many times have you thought of buying something and suddenly you notice it everywhere? Think of buying a red car and red cars are all you see on the roads. Nothing has changed except your perception. With your vision clearly in your mind, you will start to see everything from within that context and find yourself thinking 'how can this person, situation or opportunity help me towards my vision?'

- **Being more proactive**
  Rather than waiting for something to turn up, you are more able to make informed decisions and take charge, rather than being buffeted by circumstance

What should your vision be? It should be true to you and inspire you.

You might begin by going back to what originally made you become an artist (or what made you pick up this book). What was the picture you had in your mind then?

Look ahead five or ten years – where do you see yourself, who do you see yourself becoming? Looking ahead is so important because if you start building your vision from where you are now, it cannot help but be limited, because you will be thinking from a mindset of 'I can't do that because…' which is perfectly natural. So

Imagine yourself thriving in your artistic life

take away all restraints, real or imagined. Think of what your perfect, creative practice would look like and make the image as big and real as you can. Imagine yourself thriving in your artistic life.

Imagine how you will feel when you produce a finished piece or arrive at the private view of your first solo exhibition. Or maybe it is the process of drawing, sculpting, photography which is most important to you.

This unlimited vision will create a powerful pull for how you can get from your current situation to your vision. It may take years to reach but you can start making small changes and progress now.

Do you feel the pull to action?

To strengthen that pull consider creating a vision board as a constant reminder of what you want to do. Collate images and text on a sheet of paper, pinboard or in a software app like Word, Pages, Evernote or Pinterest. Make it as detailed and colourful as you like and keep it somewhere you can see it: on the wall of your studio, in the front of your sketchbook or on the home screen of your phone, laptop or tablet.

Breaking your vision into goals

When you have created your big vision, breaking it down into goals is incredibly helpful for keeping you on track and motivated. If your vision is based, for example, on where you want to be in five years, do you really want to wait that long to see how you are doing? Just like with a long physical journey when you check motorway signs or station stops to check where you are, setting goals towards your vision will help to move you forward, stay on track, assess your progress and give you a chance to pat yourself on the back.

You may have heard of SMART goals: **S**pecific, **M**easurable, **A**ction-Oriented[10], **R**ealistic, **T**imed.

Say you have a vision to become a quilter, with ideas forming in your head of incorporating quilting into mixed media compositions and installations. But how do you begin?

You could set yourself a smaller, starting goal such as 'I will learn quilting to produce a cot quilt for my niece's christening gift in six months'.

This is SMART because it is:

Specific   No one is in any doubt about what is planned

Measurable   'A cot quilt'. You need to have measures so you know when you have achieved your goal

Action-   'I will produce' is active, not just trusting
Oriented   to fate (unlike 'I will win the lottery', where you can buy a ticket and the rest is up to the vagaries of the draw)

Realistic   The timeframe and measure are realistic

---

10   *There are several versions of A in SMART goals nowadays – George T Doran, the original author used Assignable. I like Action-Orientated as it refers to doing something – I know people who have used Achievable, set achievable goals but then not actually taken any action!*

| | whilst giving leeway for the opportunity to learn and develop |
| **Timed** | Your timeframe can be any length you like, in this case six months. You might want it to fit in with a significant event, such as a birthday or when the children go to college |

Goals are there to support you and move you forward, not to beat yourself up with. If you haven't fulfilled a previous goal, check why – was it the wrong goal, was it some other circumstance, did something else happen which was actually better?

Moving from goals into action

You can have a great goal but still not feel motivated because of one major question – how do you start? This is where planning comes in. Many people fear that planning a creative project will take away all the spontaneity. But planning is just working out how to get from A to B – no one says you can't take the pretty route.

Depending on which analogy you prefer, a plan can be like a foundation, something solid on which you can dance, jump, run and play, knowing that you can always come back to standing on safe ground. Or it could be a parachute, where you can jump into the unknown, knowing that you have something to hold on to so that you don't land with a sickening thud.

Good planning involves identifying all the things which could go wrong or the excuses you may come up with and working out possible solutions in advance. It can help you to find better, more efficient or more inventive ways to approach things. It can even help you to decide if a project is actually worth doing.

Having broken your vision into SMART goals, you can break that into monthly, weekly and daily actions to get you moving.

Taking our quilting example from above, actions could include:

- Find somewhere to learn about quilting basics (online, a book, a friend)
- Decide on a design for the quilt
- Decide on hand or machine sewn (and do I need to borrow a sewing machine?)
- Decide on fabrics
- Source fabrics
- Work out how long the quilt will take to make
- Schedule how much time is needed each week to make the quilt within six months

Start by writing down all the actions you can think of and then arrange them into an order of when you need each one to happen.

Breaking a big goal down into smaller ones and celebrating the completion of each one as a triumph is a great way to stay motivated.

There's a well-known saying, 'Fail to plan, plan to fail'. I prefer to think, 'Fail to plan, be prepared to miss a lot of fascinating opportunities'.

Keep it fresh

Every few months have a review and take a fresh look at your vision. Has this changed? Is your vision still pulling you forward? Remind yourself why this vision is important to you and how you will feel when you achieve it. Check if your vision needs tweaking to keep it challenging and exciting.

Having a vision can inspire you on those days when things aren't quite going the way you want. It reminds you that whatever hasn't worked is just a temporary setback and you have a bigger, longer game to play. Managing your milestone goals and taking clear, doable actions every day will keep the motivation going.

I want it to be perfect

They happen to all of us: those times when you hold back from starting something because you want it to be perfect. You don't want to commit to paper until the composition is finished in your head, or perfectly honed. Consequently, it stays locked inside you and you never actually do the work.

If the search for perfection is blocking you, you could always take heart from the extreme actions of the following highly respected and successful artists:

Alex Katz said when he was finding his style, 'I'd do a painting a day usually. I think I destroyed about a thousand paintings by the end of my twenties'.[11]

Louise Bourgeois who, if unhappy with a sculpture, would 'shove it off the end of her kitchen table and watch it smash to smithereens'.[12]

Gerhard Richter who, at the point when he was first building his reputation, destroyed about sixty of his paintings which would now be worth millions on the art market, in what he called, 'an act of liberation'.[13] Although he is not so at odds with his work now he still cuts up work if it displeases him.

We all make what we perceive as mistakes (see "I don't want to fail"). We are human, but don't let the mistakes define you or hold you back. Embrace them, learn the lessons and move on as a more knowledgeable and experienced person.

---

11 *https://www.interviewmagazine.com/art/alex-katz*
12 *http://www.bbc.co.uk/news/entertainment-arts-33533960*
13 *http://www.spiegel.de/international/germany/his-own-harshest-critic-a-new-look-at-works-destroyed-by-gerhard-richter-a-812515.html*

Start a piece of work telling yourself that, like Katz, you will throw it away when you are finished. Say, 'I will tear this up, delete the file, the photos, when I am finished'. It takes the pressure off creating something perfect; often you will end up with material you want to keep and come back to **Don't wait for perfect. Commit, begin and let it flow** later. At other times, you may surprise yourself with something wonderful first time around.

Don't wait for perfect. Commit, begin and let it flow. Because it has taken on a physical presence doesn't mean it is finished, it is a work in progress. Or let it go as an interesting but no longer needed experiment and throw it out. You are merely following in the tradition of Katz, Bourgeois and Richter (and Jasper Johns and Francis Bacon, who were also well known for destroying their work).

I get distracted

We live in a state of actual and virtual noise, other people's agendas, never ending to-do lists, overflowing inboxes, ringing phones and social media.

We can be carried along on a tide of frenetic activity for many reasons and I think we often mistake activity of any kind for constructive work; but being busy isn't always being productive. If we work alone all day in our studios or home offices we can feel isolated and feel we need to be connected to the rest of the world at all times via the umbilical cord of wi-fi, ready to answer that Skype call, retweet that article or update our status at all times. And let's not forget FOMO – the fear of missing out.

What we are potentially missing out on is the valuable experience we are having in that moment. I remember a conversation with a client who was a visual artist but who did not enjoying visiting galleries because his mind was back in the studio and on the work he 'should' be doing, even though the trips were intended to feed his art knowledge and experience.

When we aren't concentrating fully, we can miss important pieces of information like the deadline for an art fair application, or forget if we have confirmed a meeting with a gallery. If art is the thing you love and are dedicated to then doesn't it deserve your complete attention?

Once you can manage the distractions and concentrate fully on the creative task in hand, you get into that marvellous state defined as 'flow'. This is where time flies and you forget about your cup of tea and the rest of the world as you are absorbed in the process. This can be the place where you can find the deepest satisfaction. It also allows you to acknowledge and celebrate the progress you are making after each step.

Ways you can cut down on distractions include:

- Spend ten minutes creating a picture in your mind of what it will feel like when your painting, sculpture or installation is finished and use that to motivate yourself
- Turn off all of your devices unless you are using them as a tool in the work you are doing (and even then, turn off any apps you aren't using)
- Switch on your voicemail, put your phone on airplane mode or put your phone where you can't see it (or all three!)
- Set a specific time when you will check social media or answer emails. This can be a regular time (fifteen minutes at the beginning of each day, for example), or before or after you dive into your project ('I will spend two hours painting and then I will check Instagram').
- Use a free app which stops you accessing the internet for a length of time set by you (search 'free internet blocker' to find these)
- Close your studio or office door with a polite notice stating when you will be available to callers

- If the distractions are your family, make a deal with them to leave you undisturbed for a set amount of time in exchange for you doing something with them later
- Promise yourself a treat if you stay on track for sixty minutes (or if you get the job done)
- If you work from home, take yourself into another space where you aren't tempted to do the laundry, hoover or reorganise your shelves

And don't click on that cat video; we all know where that leads!

Remember that if you immerse yourself in your creativity for a couple of hours, the world isn't going to end.

It's self-indulgent

Many artists believe that spending their lives doing something they love is selfish or 'not a proper job'. This can result in them not marketing themselves well, being reluctant to charge appropriate prices for their work or feeling guilty when their work sells well. I have worked with several clients who, when asked if they have sold their work, say, 'Yes, but it was only to friends and family' or, 'Yes, but I felt a bit guilty because I enjoyed painting it so much'. If you have ever said either of those things, the next time someone asks you if you have sold work, stop talking after 'yes'. Selling your work, to anyone, is the beginning of building your professional career your professional career and your reputation, so shouldn't be dismissed. If anyone, including your dear Aunt Minnie, has bought your work they count as art buyers (and between you and me very few people, however much they like you, will buy your work if they don't like it).

Think about the benefits you are giving to others

If you are still telling yourself it is self-indulgent, take the focus off yourself for a moment. Whether you want to create an exhibition, a film or a hand knitted tea cosy, think about the benefits you are giving to others. (This includes you feeling happy and fulfilled, making you pleasing to be around).

Even people who say they aren't interested in 'the arts' because they don't go to the theatre or to galleries and museums still listen to all kinds of music, go to the cinema, watch television, play computer games, sit on furniture, upgrade to the coolest looking phone, read picture books to their children or buy clothes. Everything is designed: some things for pure practicality, others for the pleasure given by their artistic merit.

Why don't our wardrobes contain just one pair of green wellington boots, which serve the practical necessity of keeping our feet dry and warm? Because we want the intangible benefits our footwear gives us, for example how the shoes make us feel or look, what they say about us. So we need shoe designers.

Why do we put pictures on our walls? Because they are a source of great pleasure and evoke memories and moods. People tell me how a painting at the foot of a stairwell brightens their every morning, or makes a house feel like a home. Art makes us happy, excites us, engages our attention, gives us a window onto a real or imagined world, connects us with other people when we say, 'Did you see …' and delivers hundreds of other benefits.

To demonstrate to yourself the value of your own art, try these ideas:

- Keep a list of all the testimonials and positive comments people have made about your work to read to remind you of the pleasure your work gives people
- Write a list of works you have sold or given to people. How has each one affected the person who received it? Has it connected them to a loved one, a favourite place or a memorable time? (I have a unique, handmade gold necklace I wear every day

and each time I put it on it makes me smile and feel
a bit special)

You are adding value and pleasure to the world in which
you live.

I'm too old

- Brian Dennehy, actor and winner of Golden Globe
  and Screen Actors Guild awards, turned professional
  aged thirty-nine
- Toni Morrison, author and winner of the Pulitzer
  and Nobel prizes for literature, had her first novel
  published at the age of thirty-nine
- Fashion designer Vera Wang designed her first
  wedding dress at the age of forty
- George Eliot started writing at thirty-seven and had
  her first book published at forty
- Henri Rousseau, self-taught post-impressionist
  painter, was also known as Le Douanier (the
  customs officer), the job he left aged forty-nine,
  having started painting seriously in his early forties
- John Sheehy began to paint at the age of fifty-one
  after experiencing periods of homelessness and
  mental health problems. In 2017 he had his first

solo show and in 2018, at the age of sixty-nine, the Arts Council Collection (the UK's largest national loan collection of modern and contemporary art) bought three of his paintings

- Mary Delany became a decoupage artist aged seventy-one
- American folk artist Grandma Moses started painting seriously when she was seventy-eight, after working on farms for most of her life
- Bill Traylor, an African-American artist born into slavery before becoming a sharecropper and then homeless, started drawing aged eighty-five

Just saying!

People like me don't do creative things

Many people have their creativity stifled at an early age.

Some have been encouraged to get 'sensible', steady jobs which would set them up for life with a good income and a pension at the end of it. People with very successful non-artistic careers have come to me for coaching because they were desperate to express their creativity. Some have privileged backgrounds, where money to attend cultural events is plentiful, participation in them is encouraged and links to arts contacts are easy available. However, 'proper' corporate or traditional professional careers were expected by their families and dreams of being creative could only be a hobby on the side. Louise Bourgeois's father stopped supporting her financially when at eighteen she abandoned a maths degree to study art. He only started supporting her again when she opened a print shop, a commercial venture in her father's eyes. An artistic career can be discouraged even in privileged families.

A 'get a steady job' attitude can also be seen at the other end of the economic scale, where money is scarce. There is also, I believe, still a perception among some lower income families that jobs in the arts 'aren't for people like us', perhaps because they believe they can't get into university or art or drama school, that they're not from the 'right' background or class, not rich or 'posh' or don't have the right connections. I am aware of this because I am involved with the charity Arts Emergency who create opportunities for people without privilege and aim to counter the myth that university, and in particular arts degrees, are the domain of the wealthy and well-connected.[14]

There are actually many examples of people in the arts coming from less privileged origins. Hollywood and

---

14   http://arts-emergency.org

stage actors Sir Ian McKellen, an engineer's son from Bolton, and Sir Derek Jacobi, son of a secretary and a tobacconist in Leytonstone, only got into Cambridge because they won scholarships. Both were fascinated by the theatre before that but it was at Cambridge where their talents were honed and recognised. Sir Peter Hall, also a 'classic, working-class scholarship boy', went on to become 'the single most influential figure in modern British theatre'.[15] The potter Grayson Perry was born into a working class family in Chelmsford before becoming a Royal Academician, picking up a CBE (whilst dressed as an 'Italian mother of the bride'), and being 'let in by the art-world mafia'. [16] [17]

It's true to say that the arts are generally viewed as highbrow but there are different types of art which appeal to different audiences. Artistic creations by artists, writers, musicians, designers and technicians are everywhere whether we realise it or not. Whether you like The Sex Pistols and/or Placido Domingo, Mamma Mia and/or La Boheme, Skyfall and/or Battleship Potemkin, Ikea and/or Linley, or Tiffany's and/or Claire's Accessories, creativity in some form enhances all our lives. (I say 'and/or' because yes I have both the cast

15   https://www.theguardian.com/stage/2017/sep/12/peter-hall-obituary-british-theatre-rss-national

16   https://www.telegraph.co.uk/news/uknews/honours-list/10595005/Grayson-Perry-collects-CBE-in-Italian-mother-of-the-bride-outfit.html

17   Grayson Perry, Playing to the Gallery, Particular Books, 2014

of Glee and Arvo Pärt on my iPhone). Sir Ian McKellen is equally happy working in Shakespeare, Coronation Street, X-Men, music videos, pantomime and sitcoms and he takes his audience with him.

One of the most important aspects of creativity is uniqueness. How many times have you been at an event with someone else and your individual experiences of it have been wildly at variance? This is because we all process and react to experiences through our own distinct filters, born out of our ethics, attitudes, beliefs, world view, aspirations, relationships, habits, upbringing, education and personal history. No one has exactly the same combination of life experiences as you. Whatever your background, your insights and instincts are as distinct as your fingerprints and, as this individuality and uniqueness is what fuels your unique creative talents, we all benefit if you use those talents to help us to see the world in a different way.

> One of the most important aspects of creativity is uniqueness

I'll never be as good as....

Why would you want to be like someone else? Sure, use other people as inspiration, learn from them and ask them questions. I am a great believer in picking other people's brains for insight and feedback. But the key to your creativity must surely be authenticity and if you aren't being true to yourself, people will always pick up on that. Recognise and rejoice in the fact that you bring something very special to the party. As Oscar Wilde wrote, 'Art is the most intense mode of individualism that the world has known'.[18]

Why would you want to be like someone else?

There is also something else to consider. Yes, it can be frustrating when you see someone doing something amazing without appearing to break into a sweat: Picasso painting freehand on glass, David Hockney drawing on his iPad, Louise Bourgeois creating a female figure from tangerine peel (all of which can be seen on YouTube).

You can probably show me someone you know who just picks up a pencil and creates gorgeous drawings, picks up a guitar and improvises a tune or, like my

---

18   Oscar Wilde, *The Soul of Man under Socialism*, *Fortnightly Review*, 1891

grandmother, could see someone wearing a jumper or cardigan and go home and knit it without a pattern. And I can probably show you someone who has spent years learning, practising and putting in the work and the time into their craft.

If you want to emulate your role model, forget their finished work and consider instead their behind the scenes practice and their commitment to turn up and do the work in order to reach the point where they can do what they do today.

Ideas

I have too many ideas

When I describe what I do as a coach, the comment which tends to get most reaction is when I say that I work with people who are blocked because they have too many ideas. There are bashful grins of recognition or outright declarations of, 'That's me!'

The blockages are most often caused by not knowing where to start, or a fear of following one route and it not being the 'right' one. Either way the most common result is that nothing gets done, leading to a build-up of frustration and lack of productivity.

Sometimes people think they should focus on one idea, but which one? Until you have played with an idea you can't often tell how much potential it has. Even if it turns out to be a dud, it can spark off even more ideas. The key is how to capture and deal with them all so that you don't get stuck in a state of 'paralysis by analysis'.

Here are some ideas to help move you forward:

A wall chart

Get the ideas out of your head and on to paper to get some clarity on which to follow up and when. This process involves a large sheet of paper and sticky notes.

* Lay the paper on a table or pin it to a wall
* On a sticky note, write down the essence of your first idea in a couple of words or a very short sentence and then stick it anywhere on the paper
* Do the same for every other idea until you have got them all out of your head. (Remember to only have one idea on each sticky note)
* When all of the ideas are scattered on the paper, start arranging them into a rough order of priority. (Don't stress too much about this – this is just an outline and you can fine tune later)

This process helps to:

* Get the ideas out of your head and into one place where you can see them
* Shape short, medium and long term goals
* Free you from the panic of having to do everything *now*
* Start creating some structure to move from idea into action
* Identify the priorities – the ideas you *really* want to do against the ones which would be nice if you have the time (you can move those into a 'holding pen' on one side of the paper)

You can put this up on the wall to use as a constant guide to what you want to do, and when, to keep you clear and motivated.

Plate spinning

How often have you heard someone complaining about having too many plates to spin?

Have you ever watched someone spinning plates? You can check out videos on YouTube. It is a surprisingly good analogy about being able to hold the bigger picture whilst keeping track of each project or idea.

When watching plate spinners, I noticed two things. They would start spinning the first plate, then the next one and possibly a third. Then they would go back to plate one and two to make sure they were running okay. Then they would start spinning plates four and five. Then go back and check on the first four plates, maybe giving one of them an extra boost, and so on.

The second thing I noticed was that even when checking in on a plate for a moment, it was with total focus.

How is this relevant to our plethora of creative ideas? Well, we can use the same sort of thinking when running multiple projects.

Develop a habit of checking in on your projects on a regular basis. For example, once a week take fifteen minutes or so to run through all your ideas. It isn't necessarily about *doing* any of this work (as some of the projects may have a longer timeline), but simply checking the progress of each project – are the plates still spinning or are they tottering?

This helps you identify your priorities, spot any potential problems and set goals and actions for the next stage of each project.

Develop a habit of checking in on your projects on a regular basis

Knowing the status of each project helps you focus entirely on one project 'plate' until you have that spinning safely, before moving back to the next.

Trying things on for size

Sometimes you don't follow through on an idea because you're worried you'll choose the 'wrong' thing, that the decision will be absolutely final and that you won't be able to go back on it.

Think of a new idea as a coat. Very few of us would buy a coat without trying it on to check the fit, feel the fabric, etc.

When shopping for a coat, you put on the first one and you like the length, but not the colour.

The next coat, you like the colour, but it's too tight under the arms.

The next coat, you like the collar and buttons, but the sleeves are too long.

The next coat, the colour and length are great, but you don't like the fabric.

And all the time you're trying on coats, you are getting a clearer picture of exactly what you want your coat to be like.

Use the same process to find your latest creative idea. Try things in a voluntary capacity, or a short course, or taster class, or ask a friend to teach you what they do.

Experiment and don't feel that whatever you choose first is a lifelong commitment. You can make it a game to try as many things as possible and get your friends involved and after trying on a whole wardrobe of coats, you can find a perfect fit.

So which do you want to try first – the ankle-length cashmere or the pea jacket?

I don't have any ideas

Most of us have had one of those days when we stared at the laptop, the new canvas or the piece of wood, and didn't know what to do.

But as Alex Katz put it, 'If you know what you're doing, you're doing dull stuff'.[19]

Yes, sometimes you absolutely need to know exactly

---

19   https://www.interviewmagazine.com/art/alex-katz

what you are going to do (please never, ever fly a jumbo jet without having a very clear idea of how to do it!) but when being creative you can just start and see where it goes, picking up a pencil to take a line for a walk, to paraphrase Paul Klee.

It can be very powerful to embrace the freedom of the literal or metaphorical clean page if you give yourself permission to believe that anything is possible and nothing is wrong. The brush stroke which initially seems heavy can suddenly add a whole new element you haven't seen before. The phrase which is a bit clunky can, during the process of honing, open up a whole other strand of ideas.

Even when you know your stuff, inspiration can go out of the window and no amount of yearning will bring it back. Whilst it is frustrating, it isn't wrong, it's merely part of the cycle of creation when the mind has to be left alone to percolate ideas.

Take a deep breath and trust that this moment will pass. But if you're up against a deadline and want to stimulate some ideas, here are some suggestions:

Try something different

Is it the ideas that are blocked or the way you express them? I can give you a personal example of what I mean here:

I used to sit down at my laptop every week to write

my blog, knowing the message I wanted to impart and a vague idea of how I wanted to write it. I would start typing and after an hour or so, with a bit of a struggle, I would have written my usual four hundred words.

One day when travelling I had an idea for a blog but didn't have my iPad with me. I got out my trusty notebook and pen, despite thinking it was waste of time as I was only going to have to type it all out later on, but I didn't want to lose the idea. But by the end of my forty-five minute journey, I had written *three* blogs. To say I was amazed was an understatement, but as I thought about it, I realised that when I type, I edit as I go. I start typing, then correct a sentence. Then do the same for the next one and spend ages trying to hone the perfect phrase. By the time I have done all this, I have completely lost my flow. When writing by hand I knew it was going to be edited when I typed it so was much freer in my writing and stayed in my flow.

If you are stuck or feeling unproductive why not try another medium, purely as an experiment to shake up your thinking? Who knows, it could make all the difference. For me, nearly all my writing now starts in a notebook.

Pick up a paperclip

Take an ordinary paperclip and invent as many uses for it as possible. The rule is that you can't use it to hold papers together. Now you have no choice but to look at it differently. I'll start you off:

- A toothpick
- A bookmark
- Cocktail stick

You get the idea. How many can you add to this?

What is important is not what you come up with, but the process: the taking of an object, stripping away the obvious use, bending it out of shape, turning it upside down, and coming up with as many new ways of viewing it as possible. A saucepan can become a planter (or, as any child will show you, a great hat). A glass jar becomes a pen tidy, drill bit storage, terrarium, light or photo frame. Car tyres can become coffee tables…

What you can do with objects you can do with ideas, habits or situations. If you are stuck, how many other ways can you think about the situation, when the obvious one (to you) is taken away? For example:

- You always photograph in colour – how many other filters or finishes can you find for your image?
- You always listen to classical music when you work

– what happens when you listen to hip hop or jazz?
* You always begin drawing with an HB pencil – what happens if you use chalk?

Have fun and be like a child, giving yourself the freedom of exploration they have without rules or boundaries.

Another kick starter

Here's another idea:

* Name a type of animal
* Give two words to describe the animal
* Where is the animal?
* Give two words to describe where the animal is
* What is the animal doing?
* Give two words to describe what the animal is doing

I came up with: 'A small white dog in a brown wicker basket chewing a squeaky toy'.

What did you come up with? You have just created the idea for a painting. Or add 'once upon a time' and you've started a story.

For the future, you may want to start compiling an ideas file. Build up a file of postcards, images from magazines, headlines from articles, biscuit packet wrappers, bus tickets, adverts, recipes, photos, poems… You can store these in a plastic file or a drawer or scan them into an app like Evernote. When you get stuck flick through the file for inspiration: put random ideas together, sketch ideas, look for links or look for differences.

Do something else completely

Agatha Christie is listed in the Guinness Book of Records as being the best-selling novelist of all time, so she knew a thing or two about writing. Although disciplined in her writing habits (often working on two books at a time), she said that the best time to plan a book is while you're doing the dishes. But when you are working on a creative project and hitting a block, how often do you worry at it rather than give yourself the time and permission to go off and do something else?

I admit this is a problem I have from time to time. I feel that in order to be working, I should be at my computer, on the phone or at least looking as though I am busy. This is a particularly foolish idea as I work on my own so no one sees me! My subconscious knows better though, which explains why I have notebooks and pencils in every room of the house for those moments when I am reading a book, listening to music, cooking, dusting, even asleep, when I suddenly get an idea or a fresh insight on a project. And how many of us have had our best ideas in the shower?

I have guest bloggers on my website, all creative practitioners, and looking back over their blogs I am struck by the number of times people say that when they hit a creative block they go for a walk to get away from all the distractions. Other people meditate to get back in balance. Some go fishing. Some dance around their studios.

Being strict and having a routine is very valuable in helping you to get into the mindset of working and being productive. But sometimes going off and doing something completely different is exactly what you need to get the creative juices flowing. Remember to have the notebook, sketchpad, iPad or phone to hand to capture them all.

Other People

My teachers never encouraged me

As a boy Sir Cameron Mackintosh was always putting on musical shows. He recalled how his school reports said, 'It would be really good if he paid attention to his school work instead of his other interests'.[20] Decades later, Mackintosh was quoted by the New York Times as being 'the most successful, influential and powerful theatrical producer in the world'.[21]

Closer to home, my Aunt told me she went to school with a boy, Alan, who was always drawing. His teachers told him he would never amount to anything with his doodling and he left school at fourteen. The next time my Aunt heard about Alan Aldridge was when his obituary, headed 'Artist behind some of the most striking pop images of the 1960s and 70s', appeared in the Guardian. He was dubbed by John Lennon as 'His Royal Master of Images to their Majesties the Beatles'.[22]

20   *Imagine: Cameron Mackintosh: The Musical Man, BBC Television, September 2017*
21   *http://www.nytimes.com/1990/12/09/magazine/the-musical-is-money-to-his-ears.html*
22   *https://www.theguardian.com/artanddesign/2017/feb/22/alan-aldridge-obituary*

When I was twelve, I was asked by my careers teacher what I wanted to be when I left school. At that point in my life I loved playing with photos of furniture and furnishings in magazines, cutting them out and using them to design homes so I told the teacher I wanted to be an interior designer.

'Don't be ridiculous', she said, 'There's no call for them'. In a rare act of defiance, I turned on my heel and walked out. Looking back, it probably wasn't something that I was dreadfully passionate about as I didn't follow through with it, (although having a double-barreled surname and dodgy dress sense, I could have been a female Laurence Llewelyn-Bowen). But if it had been a genuine dream of mine her words could have done real harm.

Put a positive spin on the facts

If your teachers discouraged you, how much time have you spent believing what they said? And I bet you can remember every negative comment which was made. Holding onto those comments and thoughts, from people who we regard as 'knowing better', can shape your attitudes towards yourself. I spent most of my professional life believing that I was no good at maths, all based on one throwaway comment made by a teacher when I was twelve. I ignored the fact that I had spent most of my professional life creating and managing six-figure budgets.

What can you do *now* to change the comments which were made *then*? Not a thing. But what *can* you change? You can change how you view it.

Right now, retell the story. Say it out loud as an anecdote, or write it as a short story. Put a positive spin on the facts. Make yourself the hero of the story: 'Hey, look at me now!' Then let it go.

Stop dwelling on something over which you have no control. Remember Cameron Mackintosh's and Alan Aldridge's teachers who got it so wrong.

People wouldn't like what I'd create

Louise Bourgeois studied art from the age of eighteen, worked constantly, taught, had a few shows and was part of the influential American Abstract Artists Group. But it was not until 1982, when she was seventy and given a retrospective exhibition at the Museum of Modern Art, that 'she at last took her place as queen of New York, one of the most inventive and disturbing sculptors of the century'.[23]

Vincent Van Gogh, often seen as the poster boy

---

23   https://www.theguardian.com/artanddesign/2010/may/31/ louise-bourgeois-obituary-art

for artists unappreciated during their lifetimes, was in fact building a reputation at the time of his fatal bullet wound at the age of thirty-seven. In 1890, the year of his death, he showed six paintings in Brussels and ten in the Salon des Indépendants in Paris to positive reactions from both the public and fellow artists. He sold his first piece and had a positive article on his work written by leading art critic, Albert Aurier. Had his mental state been more robust he might have lived longer to see this appreciation grow.

If your work is innovative, recognition doesn't always come quickly

Paul Cezanne was rejected by The Salon, the official art exhibition of the Académie des Beaux-Arts, every year from 1864 to 1882. He had his first solo exhibition in 1895, when he was fifty-six, at which point his work became sought after, including a purchase of one of his works by the National Gallery of Berlin in 1900. Until the last decade of his life the public was slow to appreciate his work, but he was always held in high regard by many of his esteemed contemporaries and younger artists.

These all illustrate the point that as a creative person, especially if your work is innovative, recognition doesn't always come quickly. It helps if you can be resilient and manage rejection. As an artist you create from the heart and soul and it can feel like your works are your babies, an extension of you. When someone criticises or dislikes them it can feel like a stab in the heart, a personal insult.

But step back a moment. Do you have friends who produce creative work (whether it's painting, cooking, knitting or gardening)? Do you love everything they produce? If you don't like their work, if it is not to your taste, does it stop you liking them or make you think less of them? You can't like every piece of art, television programme, piece of music or item of clothing.

Sometimes critical feedback (critical both in the sense of critique and in the sense of being important) can be very useful to hear, as it can help you to develop your ideas. However, if what you are told is counter to your style or aims, you can say politely, 'Thanks but no thanks'. Try not to take the comments personally, listen to and trust your instincts and understand that most people genuinely want to help and contribute – they may just be clumsy in their communication. I was at an artist's talk where a member of the audience explained, in detail, how the artist could have made the work 'better'; it was a potentially awkward moment for everyone. The artist didn't engage but with great politeness, calmness and sincerity said, 'Thank you for your generosity in sharing your ideas'. As Marcus Aurelius said, 'Remember that all is opinion'.[24]

---

24   *Marcus Aurelius, Meditations, Book II/15*

I realise that with something as personal as your art work this may be easier said than done. But take a breath, keep focused, don't dilute your dream and keep pushing forward. Believe in what you are trying to create even when no one else does. Learn to hold your nerve and remember why you are doing it.

I can't do it on my own

Many artists find the solitude of their work fine for a few days, but then start going stir crazy by the end of the week. This is where having support networks is so important. This can be in the form of another job, your friends and family or other artists.

You can use these support networks to meet and collaborate with other people, share ideas, create bonds, ask for help, have a moan, celebrate and generally look after your wellbeing.

You can find professional and social groups which meet regularly in networking events or you can go to other people's shows and private views. If you want to do something creative as part of a group, you can join an amateur dramatics group, a choir, a class. (I go to arts, local business and coaches networking groups plus tango classes, as well as meeting with friends).

You aren't even limited to being in the same space. Facebook groups and other online communities can expand your connections. I know a couple who are collaborating on a musical project over the net with the composer in Thailand and the lyricist in Aberdeen.

See also "Nowhere near me does what I want to do".

I don't know the right people

As in most professions there is a large element of 'it's not what you know, but who you know' in the art world. If you are serious about building a career and an income from your creative practice, other people need to know about what you do, whether they are mentors, allies, clients or potential collaborators. All of these people can spread the positive word about your work, and the more people you get to know, the more potential ambassadors you have.

If you aren't getting out there, you aren't taking control of your career

If you aren't getting out there, you aren't taking control of your career. This has all kinds of implications, not least of which is that you can't move your vision forward. For example, at a private view you could be talking to the partner of an agent who is looking for new artists, to the person who has direct contacts with the gallery where you want to see your work or be chatting with an artist who has just been reading about an open call for an exhibition which would be perfect for you.

If you haven't networked before it may seem daunting, but it's simply putting yourself in the right places to have conversations with people, either in person or online.

You can find many good sources of information online and in books about how to network, so I will only give an overview here. [25]

There are three stages of networking:

Preparation (this applies to building contacts both in person and online):
- Why do you want to network?
- Who do you want to meet?
- Where will you meet them?
- How can you find events?
- What do you want to tell people about your work?

Create a mind map of all the ideas you come up with

---

25 Try Susan Mumford and Chris King's *Art is Your Life. Make it Your Living (Be Smart About Art Publishing, 2015)* or go to https://www.creativeboom.com or http://www.thedesigntrust.co.uk

and start building a plan of action.[26] Then pick your first event.

At the event:
* Relax, be open to opportunities
* Make contact with a smile to the person nearest to you and say hello
* Start a conversation
* Move on – don't stay with one person all evening

Follow up:
* If you don't follow up and build on the relationship, then what is the point of going out and making all this effort in the first place?
* Follow up the next day or at least within forty-eight hours, whilst the meeting is still in both your minds

Take a look at arts networks such as ArtCan and Be Smart About Art to get started.[27]

Of course, you can learn how to network and still stay at home watching cat videos, or whatever your equivalent is. Here are some tips on conquering the fears which might be preventing you from going out and doing it:

---

26   *If you don't know how to mind map take a look at http://www. tonybuzan.com/about/mind-mapping*
27   *https://www.artcan.org.uk, https://www.besmartaboutart.com*

- **I feel self-conscious or embarrassed**
  Shift the focus off yourself and onto the person you are talking to by thinking, 'What can I do for them?'

- **People won't find me interesting**
  Be interested in them – you may find out all kinds of fascinating things about them which spark ideas or lead to collaborations, opportunities or future sales

- **I don't know what to say**
  Ask questions, listen to the answers and take the lead from them. Prepare a couple of lines about yourself and your work beforehand

- **I don't like crowds**
  Find smaller events and go early before it fills up. Think of any event as a group of individual people and concentrate only on the one or two who are in front of you

- **I don't know what will happen when I get there**
  Research the venue, find out who will be going, find out if there's an agenda (and see "I'm frightened" for my suggestions on what's the worst that can happen)

- **I won't fit in**

  Pick events where you will meet like-minded people

- **I get nervous**

  This is a very human reaction to things which are important to you. Here's a little tip I picked up in the days when walking into a room of strangers was one of my biggest fears. I would look for the person who seemed more nervous than me (perhaps standing off to the side of the room, maybe avoiding eye contact, or fascinated by the fire regulations on the wall), casually wander over to them and say 'hello'. Most times just that first approach will begin to relax you and the other person is usually so grateful to you that they loosen up as well so you both end up having an enjoyable evening

- **I'm not comfortable selling**

  Good networking is not about selling but about building relationships, having real conversations with real people

- **I find the conversations awkward**

  You won't necessarily 'click' with everyone you meet. If the conversation is faltering be polite, smile and say, 'It's been lovely to meet you, but I mustn't monopolise you' and move on

Incidentally, some of these tips are also relevant to when you are at your open studios or an art fair when you want to engage with the people who come to see you. They may be interested in your work but are worried about being 'sold to' or being pounced upon. Acknowledge them with a smile, say 'hello' and give them space to look at your work. If you need a conversation starter, ask them what their interest is in art.

You won't necessarily like everyone you meet but the more people you meet the more likely it is that you will find your next client, new friends or potential collaborators and a wider, more rewarding support system.

Knowledge

I don't know how

We are learning all the time, from the moment we arrive in the world until we shuffle off this mortal coil. Whether you are taking formal classes or learning by observing how others do things, learning is a process which at its best never ends. We are learning lessons every day from the momentous to the small: how to be a parent, have a healthy relationship, apply for a mortgage, drive a car, unblock a sink, play chess or sew on a button.

When learning, we naturally come from a place of not knowing

When learning, we naturally come from a place of not knowing. As Vincent van Gogh said, 'But I keep on making *what I can't do yet* in order to learn to be able to do it'.[28]

Trying anything new will take you through a period of uncertainty, frustration and perplexity. But if you are

---

28   *Letter to Anthon van Rappard August 1885 http://vangoghletters.org/vg/letters/let528/letter.html*

committed to the outcome and take your time you will enjoy the journey and enjoy the sense of satisfaction as you learn. (And if you embrace the experience, not knowing can reap rewards and knowledge beyond your imagination – see "I don't want to fail" and "I want it to be perfect").

You can begin the learning process by:

- Watching online tutorials
- Reading books
- Signing up for a course
- Asking your friends
- Visiting galleries
- Trying taster sessions
- Checking noticeboards

If you can't commit to going to a regular class, try a one day, weekend or one week intensive course, to get a good foundation and then carry on as and when you can with suitable follow up classes.

In which other ways could you learn? Be creative!

I'm creative, not business minded

One area where my artist clients often go into freefall is around business because of the perception that creative and business brains are so different.

The theory is that the left brain deals with maths, words, facts and logic and the right brain is imaginative, creative, visual and intuitive. A two year long academic research project showed that whilst this theory is technically correct, people themselves are not predominantly left or right brained. [29] The whole brain works together to allow us to do everything. Think about it - you may create an intuitive, imaginative painting but you had to plan to have the materials and the time and get to your studio… Consider all of the times when you are spurred by emotion to create, but when you still have to bring in the practical to make it happen.

One of my aims as a coach is to teach clients how the skills you need to plan and manage a business are in fact the same as those needed to go about your daily life.

If you don't believe this, here's an example I give in my workshops:

29   *An Evaluation of the Left-Brain vs. Right-Brain Hypothesis with Resting State Functional Connectivity Magnetic Resonance Imaging http://journals.plos.org/plosone/article?id=10.1371/journal. pone.0071275*

You live in South East London (A) and you have to travel to North West London (B) to arrive by eleven o'clock on a Monday morning. Quickly list the first three things you think of that you need to do to get from A to B.

You could have said: work out the best route, check the timetable, check you have enough money for the fare or enough petrol in the tank, arrange childcare and dozens of other things.

Whatever answers you gave, congratulations, you are now entering the world of business planning.

This is a very simplistic example and obviously there are things you need to understand about income, expenditure, etc but business planning is just planning, creating the route to take you from where you are now to where you want to be.[30]

Business jargon often flummoxes people, but even then just because you don't know the terms doesn't mean that you don't know the process. For example, I ran a workshop with professional artists and asked how many knew what the brokerage revenue model was. Blank faces all around. I explained it was how galleries and most art fairs work: the artist gives the gallery the painting, the gallery brokers a deal with

---

30   *You will find my free ebook, Demystifying the Business Planning Process, which sets out some first steps on my website www. catchingfireworks.co.uk/free-resources*

the art collector, then splits the income with the artist. There was a collective 'aah' of recognition in the room because all of them were doing this on a regular basis, they just hadn't come across the business term. Take heart – few bankers would know what a giclée print is!

In the same way that you learn anything, you can get to grips with jargon by finding people who can teach you, joining classes (in person or online), reading books and asking for advice. I use a tool called the Business Model Canvas in my workshops, a single page listing all of the areas you need to work on to run a business. [31] When I introduce this to delegates they are often surprised at how much they already have in place. And if you can use Google maps (other maps are available!) or travel websites to help you with your physical journey, you can use accountancy software, social media and coaches to help you in your professional one.

I just can't get started

You have the skills, the experience and the equipment and yet you are stuck.

When asked about how to deal with creative blocks composer Stephen Sondheim said that if faced with

---

31   https://strategyzer.com/canvas/business-model-canvas

a blank sheet of paper you should write something, anything, even if it is just, 'Cat, cat, cat, cat, cat...' because this gets the thinking process started.

In her book The Creative Habit Twyla Tharp talks about how as a novice choreographer she didn't know how to start a dance, so she took a deep breath, stamped her foot on the sprung wooden floor and shouted, 'Begin'.[32] This led directly to creating a dance, The Fugue, which was performed in silence on an electronically amplified floor.

Plan your day the previous evening – write down the three key things you want to achieve the next day, however big or small. Consider getting an accountability buddy – tell someone what you are planning to do, and get them to send you a text the next morning to remind you or to find out if you have done it. Or, as some artists do, end your working day leaving a small mundane job to go back to the next day. It gets you into action as soon as you arrive in your studio and gives you time for your mind to wander, cooking up new ideas.

When you don't know what to do, which action you take isn't important. Simply take action, any action. You never know where it might lead.

You might also want to read "I don't have any ideas".

---

32   Twyla Tharp, The Creative Habit, Simon & Schuster, 2006

Logistics

Nowhere near me does what I want to do

When you want to learn or develop your support system it can be frustrating to find nothing is available to you, but you could set up something yourself.

Examples I have seen include:

- Life drawing classes – a couple of artists wanting to hone their life drawing skills put the word out and found a few other artists who wanted to do the same. They all chipped in some money to hire a model once a month for a class in one of their studios

- A gallery group – a group of artist friends go to a gallery or museum once a month. Each person takes a turn to choose the venue and do pre-visit reading to brief the others. They get group rates on entry fees. Their responses to what they have seen inspires their own work

- A book group – set up by artists to read business and art books, they meet monthly to discuss what they have read and support each other to take action

These were set up by personal contact and through Facebook and Twitter.

If you think something is missing in your area, there is a very big chance someone else is thinking exactly the same thing. Put the word out and join forces.

I don't have the space

How much space do you need? This is a serious question. If you are lucky, you have a spare room which you can use as a study, studio or hobbies room. Perfect. But being space poor does not have to stop you. If you look at it objectively with an open mind you can do lots with a limited space.

I know of:

- A professional artist whose studio is on her (smaller than average sized) landing
- A filmmaker whose editing suite is under the stairs
- A crafter who 'books' the dining table every Sunday evening
- A writer who works in his camper van on his drive

Agatha Christie didn't have a study until late in her career so often worked at a dining table with her portable typewriter. Author Cynan Jones writes in his mother's garden shed. [33]

Is there a local venue which has space you can use for free? Or which you could use in exchange for a skills swap, such as volunteering your admin skills in exchange for time in a dark room, a foundry or a studio?

Be inventive with storage. Use a seed tray to organise cluttered drawers, hang things on a wall using a pegboard or coat rack, attach lids of screw top glass jars to the underside of shelves, stick picture hooks on the inside of cupboard doors, use a paper towel holder to stack masking and gaffer tapes.

Use your imagination to find and create your space. It may not be perfect but if it allows you to keep creating it's better than no space at all. And I am sure you can always find room for the artists' most essential tools, a small sketchbook and a pencil.

---

33   *http://www.bbc.co.uk/news/uk-wales-41513441*

Finances

I can't afford to leave my job

If you have a full-time job making the leap from financial security to being a full-time artist is scary. It is hard, there are no guarantees of success and you have to do almost everything for yourself as a freelancer. You may have to start by doing some jobs for free to build up your contacts. (This is not confined to art – most stand-up comedians have to do an apprenticeship of unpaid or poorly paid gigs whilst they build their craft and reputation).

Do you have to give up your job?

Do you have to give up your job? See "I have a full-time job" for a list of famous artists who had fulfilling and successful creative careers whilst in full-time employment. This is a valid choice if you need the income or if you like your job. But make it a genuine choice rather than a reason not to pursue your artistic goals. Build a creative practice by ring-fencing time and resources to give you a balanced life.

You could create a portfolio career. Many artists mix time in their studios with work in art consultancy, teaching, art therapy, leading workshops or arts administration. This is not only for financial reasons, but also because they want the stimulation of working with other people to stave off the feelings of isolation of working alone in a studio, or for the contacts and experience it can give them.

Review your living costs, how you currently spend your income and what you may already have in place. When I wanted to leave a steady and well-paid job to start my own business I didn't believe I could afford it. I did a financial review where I discovered that although I was spending all of my monthly income, I actually needed less money than I thought to cover my essential outgoings. I was buying things I didn't need because I was unhappy in my job and I wanted to cheer myself up.

What costs do you have simply because you work full-time? Lunches out, smart clothes for an office role (and the associated dry cleaning costs), takeaways in the evening because you're too tired to cook, expensive weekends away to relax?

A financial review is an important activity at the best of times, but especially so when you are considering a change in your life. This may not be the moment to make the leap, but you might find it is closer than you think and you can begin to make plans accordingly.

In the meantime, if you can't make a big change straight away, don't despair or use it as an excuse not to continue with your dream. Review your finances on a regular basis as this helps you to keep track of all your outgoings and possibly find opportunities to save money towards a 'leaving fund'. For example, when your mobile phone or broadband contract ends, move straight away to a cheaper deal or provider. Council tax is usually split into ten monthly payments, so can you save the money from the two 'free' months? Small amounts will build up over time, helping you to keep the momentum going and to have a timeline for leaving.[34]

I can't afford the equipment

Are you genuinely stumped because you haven't got the right materials or piece of equipment? We can all let ourselves off the hook from doing our work, creative or otherwise, because we don't have the exact supplies we think we need.

Obviously, there are times when you need a kiln, a camera or a canvas (or, if you are David Hockney, an iPad). However, when you hit a block due to a lack of materials it could be an opportunity for some creative thinking. In Grayson Perry's Tomb of the Unknown

---

34   *For more ideas on budgeting, check out What's Your Excuse for not Being Better with Money? by Jo Thresher, WYE Publishing, 2017*

Craftsman exhibition there was a small, fascinating sculpture which Perry says was 'a model tower I made from detritus on my kitchen table in 1983'.[35] This was not an artistic decision, but one made due to lack of money for materials coupled with a passionate desire to make.

Author Edith Wharton says that as a child she wanted to write but 'it was not thought necessary to feed my literary ambitions with foolscap, and for lack of paper I was driven to begging for the wrappings of the parcels delivered at the house. After a while these were regarded as belonging to me, and I always kept a stack in my room. It never occurred to me to fold and cut the big brown sheets, and I used to spread them on the floor and travel over them on my hands and knees, building up long parallel columns of blank verse headed "Scene: A Venetian palace" or "Dramatis Personae" (which I never knew how to pronounce)'.[36]

I once had a conversation with a steward at an art fair. I asked if she was an artist herself and then asked her, 'In which medium?' She replied, 'It varies, depending on what I can afford'.

I loved this answer. Obviously, a more satisfactory answer could have been something like, 'I work in bronze

---

35   https://www.theguardian.com/artanddesign/2011/sep/17/
grayson-perry-tomb-craftsman-museum
36   Edith Wharton, A Backward Glance, Everyman, 1993

because I sell enough work to pay for the materials and foundry space'. But a far worse answer would have been, 'I'm not doing anything at the moment as I can't afford the materials'.

'It varies, depending on what I can afford' is a real creative's answer. If money were available, she would be working in Italy with bronze; when it's not she works in her bedroom using paper clips and paper cups.

I hate the whole concept of poor, starving creatives living hand to mouth. It perpetuates the stereotype that artists can't earn enough to live (even in the minds of the artists themselves). However I love a commitment to the idea that creativity is not dependent on money but a force, an energy in itself. It's that thing which sees one person always with a camera in his hand, another with a sketchbook and another with a notebook. Or with a pencil and a napkin if that is all that is available.

> Creativity is not dependent on money but a force, an energy in itself

After all the necessary bills have been paid, look at how else you spend your money. Do you need your skinny latte every day or could you save that money towards materials?

Have a declutter – what have you already got

which you can reuse? What can you sell? What can you swap?[37]

You don't always have to invest in the best before your start. Buy cheap pencils and paper from a pound shop, cut up old clothes or sheets to experiment with quilting or play with the camera on your Smartphone.

Who do you know who already does what you want to do? Can you borrow their kit? Can you do a skill swap?

Money may be scarce, but your creativity is always in abundance.

---

37   For help with this check out *What's Your Excuse for not Clearing Your Clutter?* by Juliet Landau-Pope, WYE Publishing, 2018

Time

I don't have the time

Put down this book, pick up a pen and doodle for two minutes. You don't need hours to create something!

When my clients say they don't have time, I often recommend the following exercise:

Work on a project for ten very focused minutes. What use is ten minutes? It's manageable and not too alarming. It's also surprising what you can do in ten focused minutes: create a sketch, write a fifty word story, read a blog, watch a video, identify resources needed or get clear on next steps.

When you use ten minutes in this way, one of two things will happen:

- If you work for the promised ten minutes and then stop you will feel good because you have kept your word with yourself. You have started, so it is now a project in progress rather than that thing you are going to get around to one day. When you come back the next day, even if only for another promised ten minutes, there are ten minutes less to do

- On the other hand, once you've got started you may go on to spend longer on the project, knowing that you can stop at any time you want and anyway, you might as well carry on now that you have started. Often you find once you begin, the job takes less time than you expected

Either way you have made a start and demonstrated to yourself that even when made up of lots of well-focused ten minutes, you *do* have the time.

I don't know how to manage my time

You have too many ideas, too much to do and not enough time to do it. In a world where we are always busy (or feel that we must always be seen to be busy), this is a common problem.

I recommend using the Five Ds to organise yourself: Do, Diminish, Defer, Delegate or Dump.

Categorise everything you have to do as follows:

- **Do it**
  We all have things on our to-do list which we don't like doing. But as the saying goes, if it's your job

to eat a frog, it's best to do it first thing in the morning and nothing worse will happen to you the rest of the day. The more you put it off, the bigger the worry (and the guilt) becomes, overshadowing everything else which you're doing. I'm a great believer in rewards so follow a rotten job with a treat or a job you will enjoy!

- **Diminish it**

  If you don't know how to start, or the job seems too big, break it into manageable pieces. How do you eat an elephant? One mouthful at a time. See also "I don't have the time"

- **Defer (Diarise) it**

  Deferring is forward planning. Block out regular times in your diary for jobs which happen every week or month (for example, a monthly newsletter, accounts) or for dealing with ongoing tasks such as emails. You can do this at the beginning of the week and make appointments with yourself, as though you are a client – you wouldn't cancel on them, so why cancel on yourself?

- **Delegate it**

  Initially, if you're starting out, you may have to do everything yourself. Whilst you are a one man band keep a list of all the jobs you would like to stop doing and look for opportunities to pass them on so you can get more time for your creative work. Or delegate the personal chores – getting a cleaner has revolutionised the professional lives of quite a few of my clients

- **Dump it**
  You might feel nervous about this one, but just because something has been written down it is not set in stone. Things change and that great idea you had a couple of months ago may not be relevant any more. Perhaps the moment has passed or something better has turned up. Maybe it is on your list because someone else suggested it and isn't yours to do at all. If the task doesn't further or contribute to your goals, delete it

Things don't always go to plan – stuff happens and however good your planning there will always be unanticipated tasks. However if you get into the habit of using the five Ds regularly you have a tool which will help you stay on top of your to-do list and help you to feel in control of your time whatever happens.[38]

---

38   *If you need more help on getting organised and being more productive, I can recommend Juliet Landau-Pope's book What's Your Excuse for not Being More Productive? (WYE Publishing, 2017)*

I have too many other things to do

Juggling multiple projects is something we all do and it's generally a good problem to have: you have a busy life with lots to stimulate you.

In your career there are projects, clients and your own professional development to manage. In your personal life there could be a partner, children, housework, gardening, friends, elderly parents, friends, charity work or DIY, all of which take up your time.

If you feel stretched to breaking point and can't find time for your own art, try this exercise. You can do this in one sitting, or in chunks of time:

Make a list of everything you do. Include absolutely everything you can think of.

Organise the list into these columns:

1   Things you like and want to do
2   Things which nurture you
3   Things which drain you
4   Necessary tasks
5   Things which seem to have landed on your plate without you noticing
6   Things which you do out of habit

Now work your way through columns 3 to 6. What you can delegate? What can you say 'no' to? Where can you negotiate? With necessary tasks, for example, is there a way you can do them differently to give you more time? Can you make better use of time built around other activities (concentrating time in the studio between taking and collecting the children from school, catching up on social media whilst waiting for a train, reading or sketching on the tube)? And with each potential change you identify, how much extra time will that give you to 'spend' on columns 1 and 2?

Some tasks may appear in more than one column. For example, a necessary task may also be one which you like and want to do, or one which drains you. Try as much as you can to work out the most relevant single column for each task – this process in itself can help you focus and work out what to do next.

Rather than trying to change everything at once, work on one area at a time and make gradual changes to adjust the balance. Each change will help you to feel more in control and less stressed and will create more pockets of time for your creative work.

It would take me too long

In this age of instant gratification some things still take time, like creating an orchard, cultivating a new species of rose or producing a fine single malt whiskey.

As Abraham Lincoln said, 'We shall sooner have the fowl by hatching the egg than by smashing it'.[39]

> How will you feel when those years have passed?

Sometimes we know how long it will take to learn a new set of skills. Without patience, if you know it's going to take years to learn something you may just not start. But how will you feel when those years have passed and you look back and think, 'I could have done it by now'? As one of my clients put it, 'If it takes me until I'm fifty I'm going to be fifty anyway'.

Looking five or ten years ahead or to the next new year can be useful. Setting a goal to be reached by your next birthday or a 'big' birthday immediately creates a more meaningful timeframe.

It takes most babies about one thousand hours of practice from the time they pull themselves upright to the time they can walk alone.[40] Building a successful artistic career is a long game too so try to enjoy the

---

39 *White House speech of 11 April 1865*
40 *http://www.parenting.com/article/learning-to-walk*

process of developing, refining and expanding your skills and knowledge.

And if it all seems to be too much effort and not something you feel you can manage don't forget that if you've ever been a baby you've already done it once.

If you are worried about how old you will be when you've finished learning, see "I'm too old".

I have a full-time job

Philip Larkin, named in 2008 by The Times as Britain's greatest post-war riter, wrote the majority of his poetry whilst working full-time as a university librarian.

L S Lowry created most of his art in the evenings while working as rent collector and chief cashier with the Pall Mall Property Company. He has an art gallery named in his honour in Salford Quays and was offered a knighthood (which he rejected).

Although Paul Gauguin became a full-time artist in his mid-thirties, he was a very successful stockbroker for eleven years prior to that, with his art as an important side project. During that period he earned as much money through his art as through his financial dealings.

Fiona Mozley wrote her 2018 Man Booker shortlisted debut novel Elmet on her phone whilst commuting. 'To get it finished I just had to take it one sentence at a time, whenever I could'.[41]

One of my clients uses the first hour of his day to sort and edit photos taken the previous day; another uses the time before everyone else wakes up to watch videos on YouTube to learn about embroidery.

If mornings aren't your thing, what about your lunch hour? How could you use that time to further your creative goals? Take a walk with a sketchbook or camera, research exhibition opportunities or get inspiration from other people's work online.

Some companies have set up arts or crafts workshops at lunchtime, understanding how this can re-energise people so that they go back to their desks refreshed and ready for the rest of the day. Perhaps this is something you could set up – it doesn't need to cost money. Bring people together with their own projects, giving each other support.

If you are a night owl you are following in the footsteps of Toulouse-Lautrec, Franz Kafka, Bob Dylan, Thomas Wolfe and Glenn Gould, to mention but a few. Find a course online which you can do at your own time and pace; no one says you can't paint or manage your accounts at three in the morning!

---

41   *https://www.standard.co.uk/lifestyle/london-life/fiona-mozley-i-wrote-a-novel-on-my-commute-now-it-might-win-the-man-booker-prize-a3598686.html*

Play with your timetable. Find the best times for you and how that can fit in with your other obligations. Where can you schedule a regular time for your creative work, time which you will not change for anything other than emergencies or illness? Block out chunks of time when you can get stuck into your work. Look for opportunities to grab the odd ten minutes when you can sketch: over a sandwich at lunchtime or while waiting for a call centre to answer the phone. Like Fiona Mozley be creative on your commute. Remember to place your creativity on an equal footing with all of your other obligations rather than treating it as an afterthought. It may take longer to build a reputation and a creative practice than if you were working on your art full-time, but you have the benefit of financial security whilst experimenting and learning your craft.

Place your creativity on an equal footing with all of your other obligations

I need to be concentrating on my other career

As discussed at the beginning of this book, success as

an artist is whatever you want it to be and for you it may not be spending five days every week in your studio. Indeed, some artists who are successfully exhibiting and selling their work still choose to have another full-time career alongside their artistic practice. Reasons for this might include the love of the other work they are doing, the need for the routine and social interaction or having an additional opportunity to build a network of contacts or to gain different experience and knowledge which enhances their artistic practice. Their alternative career may even be in a creative profession (such as a graphic designer with an artistic practice in fine art). The financial security might mean that you are not artistically compromised by commercial restraints and/or financial concerns and one of my artist clients says that she gets all of her best creative ideas when doing something totally different.

> Your creative talents and attitude can actually enhance another career

If however you feel that art is a distraction from your other career, consider that your creative talents and attitude can actually enhance another career, and enable you to make off-beam and innovative connections. Like in 1941 when Swiss engineer and inventor George de Mestral noticed the burrs sticking to his dog's fur after walks in the woods. After many years of investigation he invented Velcro.[42]

As another example, I run workshops and originally I would write whole presentations down so that I knew exactly what was going to happen every minute. Obviously, preparation is very important because unless you are an improv performer, you can't expect people to pay to watch you making it up as you go along. However, writing out every word did not leave a great deal of space for interaction and the joyous, spontaneous insights which often come out of workshops.

I knew this was a problem and tried to solve it by going down the conventional routes: reading a book or going on a course. But the answer came to me when I was dancing the Argentine Tango. Although there are individual tango steps which are learnt, the dance is completely improvised, based on factors such as the connection you have with your partner, the music and how much room you have on the dance floor. It occurred to me that this was how to run workshops; the learnt steps are the essential preparation, the music is the structure of the workshop and my partner(s) are the workshop participants. I am a reasonable dancer and being able to take the confidence of my dance skills and apply them to workshop presentation has completely

---

42   https://www.velcro.com/blog/2016/11/an-idea-that-stuck-how-george-de-mestral-invented-the-velcro-fastener

changed and improved my approach.

Have you found the answer to a business problem whilst concentrating on a creative task?

How could you use your creative skills to improve and enhance your other career?

I'll get around to it someday

In an article in The Guardian, a nurse who counselled terminal patients in their final days listed their top five regrets:

- I wish I'd had the courage to live a life true to myself, not the life others expected of me
- I wish I hadn't worked so hard
- I wish I'd had the courage to express my feelings
- I wish I had stayed in touch with my friends
- I wish that I had let myself be happier[43]

In a perfect world we would all die in comfortable old age after a happy, full life. We would have had time to do all the things we want, to be all the things we want to be. But life is unpredictable and we may not have

---

43   https://www.theguardian.com/lifeandstyle/2012/feb/01/top-five-regrets-of-the-dying

the time we think. Sometimes we let our fears hold us back. Fears of looking foolish, of the unknown, of what people will think, of not being good enough, of not knowing, of failure… But what can be a bigger failure than not living life, your only life, to the full?

There will be some instances where it's not possible to do something now, like going swimming in the middle of a shark feeding frenzy or flying in heavy fog. But often we put things in our own way which might seem sensible but which are only obstacles because we say they are.

Think about the creative project you want to do, whether it is staging an exhibition, learning to sculpt, writing a book or going on photography safari. Instead of thinking about doing it, I invite you to come at it from a different angle. Think about not doing it. Think about reaching the end of your life, which could be in fifty years or who knows when and not having done that thing you really want to do. If that doesn't worry you, then as you were.

However, if it upsets you to think of not achieving your ambition, what is the first action you can take to make it happen? Start that painting, find that class, research your flights.

Whatever that first action is, take it. Now.

Some Final Thoughts

We can spend so much of our lives worrying about and anticipating the worse. We have so much drive to create and yet we still create obstacles in our own minds. To quote Leonardo da Vinci, 'The greatest deception men suffer is from their own opinions'.[44] Obstacles can be overcome.

I hope this book has demonstrated several things:

Firstly, as you look through the excuses and recognise those which are 'yours', realise that you are not alone. We all have fears, worries, attitudes which get in our way however much we want to move forward.

Realise that you are not alone

Secondly, that it has shown you that where and who you are now is fine and exactly the right place from which to make the next moves, however small, towards creating the fulfilling artistic life you imagine for yourself. You don't have to change who you are, just bring out more of the best of yourself.

Thirdly, yes, there are external things which can slow you down, but there is so much over which you do have control if you alter your attitudes and outlook. It is not the fears and excuses themselves but how we deal with them that matters. You might not be able

44   *The Notebooks of Leonardo da Vinci, Book XIX, Jean Paul Richter, 1883*

to change all of the circumstances of your life but as
Victor E Frankl, psychiatrist and Holocaust survivor said,

Success is
whatever you
want it to be

'Everything can be taken
from a man but one
thing: the last of human
freedoms – to choose
one's attitude in any

given set of circumstances, to choose one's own way'.[45]

Fourthly, success is whatever you want it to be.

So what next?

For starters, have compassion for yourself. We are
facing scary, unknown, new situations all the time in
our lives and careers. We push ourselves to do and learn
new things. We develop our skills and put ourselves on
the line on a regular basis. It is hardly surprising that
sometimes we pull up short and think, 'Not again, I
don't want to be pushed and challenged, I just want to
take a break'.

I am not saying this to give you a get out of jail free
card or to let you off the hook, only to highlight that
these thoughts occur to many of us. You are not bad,
weak, feeble, stupid (all words which my clients have
used about themselves) but just wonderfully, gloriously
human.

---

45   Victor Frankl, *Man's Search For Meaning, Washington Square
Press,1959*

However, to grow, develop and take control of our careers we know we can't always stay in our comfort zones. Some people are 'all or nothing', working best when throwing themselves wholeheartedly into a new experience; others are more cautious, building up confidence with small, regular wins. Whether you crash out of your comfort zone like a juggernaut, or edge out of it bit by bit, both ways are equally valid, both require bravery. And both require getting into action because out of our comfort zone we must go to thrive and be successful.

Many of our excuses stem from self-sabotage. As collage artist Anthony Zinonos said, 'The inner critic is like that old friend from school that you wish would just leave you alone, but keeps calling and leaving messages'.[46] But like that old friend, you don't have to listen to it or take its advice.

Here is a final exercise you can use in conjunction with the other exercises and tips in this book: Catch It, Check It, Change It.[47]

Catch It

Catch yourself when you are having a negative thought, when you hear yourself saying words like 'can't',

---

46   Danielle Krysa, *Creative Block*, Chronicle Books, 2014
47   *This is part of CBT – if you'd like to read more about this I recommend Cognitive Behavioural Therapy for Dummies, John Wiley & Sons, 2010*

'shouldn't', or if you are feeling a bit anxious or nervous.

Check It

Listen to the negative thought. Is it factually true? Is it how someone else would see the situation or see you? What evidence do you have to prove what you say? Does the negative thought support you? Be as objective as possible. (This isn't always easy, as we always think our thoughts are true, but practice will help).

Change It

Change your negative thought for a positive one. Make it realistic and look for evidence to support it. Notice how it feels – are you feeling happier, calmer, more positive? Keep that positive thought in your mind and your mind will begin to believe it.

In the short term, it may take you a few minutes to go through this process. However as you practise it will become second nature whenever a fear or negative thought occurs. This tool can get you through a one-off situation but longer term, the more you interrupt your negative thoughts and start having positive conversations with yourself, the more confident you will feel.

All of the ideas, tips and exercises in this book are intended to help you to change your mindset and find your own solutions. Work through them, try them out, experiment with them. Use the ones which work and discard the ones which don't. Add your own ideas. Play and create.

Build a network around you, enrol people in your vision and allow them to support and nurture you.

Become more aware of where you spend and use time. It is a finite resource. Once it is gone, it is gone and there is no getting it back. It is also one of the few ways in which we are all equal, each of us having sixty minutes in an hour, twenty-four hours in a day.

Believe in yourself and keep true to your artistic practice because it is your authentic self. You know how the act of creation contributes to your mental and emotional wellbeing. Don't stop because you think it is selfish – it is taking care of yourself: would you stop wearing a plaster cast for a broken leg?

And you know what? It is important to the rest of us too. All of us need your imagination to stimulate our thinking, to educate us, to delight us, to provoke us, to make us laugh and to make our hearts sing.

So I urge you to do whatever it takes to be at your best, at your most creative and at your most thriving –

not only will you be creating a fulfilling, satisfying and happy life for yourself, but also enhancing the lives of many, many others.

Acknowledgements

My thanks to Joanne Henson for approaching me with the idea for this book and for giving me the opportunity to be part of this marvellous series (and to Kay Henson for suggesting me). Writing it has been a pleasure, a challenge and a tremendously rewarding experience.

Thanks also to four artists: Sharon Baker, Executive and Personal Coach of Fly Don't Walk; Kate Enters, Founder and Director of ArtCan; Sarah Hartley-Edwards; and Christine Manderla, all of whom read the book in its early draft stages and gave me excellent, incredibly helpful feedback. Their generosity of time, experience and insight has been essential in the process of completing the book.

Thanks to my clients for contributing all of the excuses and for their part in making my vocation a reality. I have defined my own meaning of success and I am living it every day: I couldn't do it without your trust and commitment.

Also thanks to my friends and family for putting up with me going on about 'the book' for months!

And finally, thanks to all the artists whose creativity gives us new ways to view, enjoy and understand the world, and who bring colour and joy into our lives.

About the Author

Deborah Henry-Pollard, BA Humanities (Hons) and MAC (Member of the Association of Coaching), is a certified coach working with creative professionals. She has over thirty-five years' experience of creating strategies across the arts, charity and retail sectors.

Deborah set up her business Catching Fireworks® in 2009 to concentrate on coaching, working with people who are serious about making a change in their creative life, however big or small, and want to get into action. This could be through finding ways of working which support their practice or helping them get through blocks caused by a lack of confidence, negative perceptions or unhelpful attitudes.

She is also a creative specialist with Be Smart About Art and a board member for ArtCan, a non-profit, international arts organisation which supports artists through profile raising activities and exhibitions, an open network of 'likeminded' peers and practical support structures.

Index

Also in this series

What's Your Excuse for not Being More Productive?

Juliet Landau-Pope
Overcome your excuses, stop procrastinating, get things done

Do you struggle to organise your time? Do you spend too much time planning and not enough time doing? Or are you simply unable to get started with things? Then this is the book for you.

Professional organiser Juliet-Landau Pope takes a look at all of the things you might be telling yourself to explain why you're not being as productive as you'd like, and offers practical advice, ideas and inspiration to help you move forward.

Don't know where to start? Don't have the time? Or do you simply feel overwhelmed? This supportive and motivational book will help you to tackle all of those beliefs and many more so that you can use your time more effectively in order to *get things done*.

Paperback – ISBN 978-0-9956052-2-0
e-book – ISBN 978-0-9956052-3-7

Also in this series

What's Your Excuse for not Clearing Your Clutter?

Juliet Landau-Pope
Overcome your excuses, simplify your life, make space for what matters

Do you struggle with clutter in your life? Do you feel overwhelmed by "stuff", have no space to work on new projects, or feel unable to relax? Then this is the book for you.

Decluttering expert Juliet-Landau Pope takes a look at the things which might prevent you from tackling the clutter in your life and offers practical advice, simple ideas and inspiration to help you take back control of your living space.

Not sure where or how to start? Too emotionally attached to your possessions? Holding on to things "just in case"? Overcome your excuses, tidy up your life, feel calmer and more organised and make space for new projects and experiences.

Paperback – ISBN 978-0-9933388-4-4
e-book – ISBN 978-0-9933388-5-1

Also in this series

What's Your Excuse for not Being Better With Money?

Jo Thresher
Overcome your excuses and get to grips with your personal finances

Do you wish you could be savvier with money but find it too daunting? Do you wish you were more in control of your finances but find yourself avoiding taking action? Then this is the book for you.

Personal finance expert Jo Thresher takes a look at all of the reasons you might give for not getting to grips with your money, and offers advice, ideas and inspiration to help you change that.

No time to get organised? Scared to look at your bank statement? Think you're a shopaholic? Not money minded? Overcome all of these excuses and many more. Improve your relationship with your cash and feel more secure, more relaxed and more in control.

Paperback – ISBN 978-0-9956052-0-6
e-book – ISBN 978-0-9956052-1-3

Also in this series

What's Your Excuse for not Being More Confident?

Charlotta Hughes
Overcome your excuses, increase your confidence, unleash your potential

Do you feel you could achieve much more in life if only you had more confidence? Do you know you'd be happier if you were braver, or had more self-belief? Then this is the book for you.

In this supportive and motivational book former Life Coach of the Year Charlotta Hughes takes a look at all of the ways in which we hold ourselves back and avoid expanding our horizons and she offers advice, ideas and inspiration to help change things.

Scared of failure? Feel unappreciated? Hate change? Worried about what others might think? This book will help you overcome all of your excuses and give you the motivation you need to change the way you feel about yourself.

Paperback – ISBN 978-0-9933388-8-5
e-book – ISBN 978-0-9933388-9-2

Lightning Source UK Ltd.
Milton Keynes UK
UKHW02f1147110918
328697UK00003B/20/P